THE JOURNEY CONTINUES VOL.4 PSALMS A REFLECTION OF GOD'S HEART

WILLIAM HATFIELD

ACKNOWLEDGEMENTS

We are all on a journey through life! I want to thank all my family and friends who stand besides me and encourage me when times are tough.

I especially want to thank my aunt Viola for all her work in editing and preparing the manuscript of my first book for publishing. The knowledge she shared will help me to continue writing. Her confidence in me ignited a gift I never realized I had. God created me with many gifts and one of them is to be a writer. Thank you Jesus for your great love.

DEDICATION

I dedicate this book to the thirsty and hungry saints of God that desire an intimacy with the Holy Spirit like no other. My prayer is that you can find this journey as a source of encouragement, strength and power to overcome life's struggles and walk in a greater sense of freedom and relationship with the Holy Spirit and all within your sphere of influence.

PROLOGUE

THE HOLY SPIRIT COMMUNICATES TO US IN A VARIETY OF WAYS. I HAVE FOUND PSALMS OR

PROPHETIC POETRY ENCOURAGING AND VERY HELPFUL WITH MY RELATIONSHIP WITH JESUS. I PRAY THESES PSALMS MAY BE AS ENCOURAGING TO YOU AS THEY ARE TO ME.

CONTENTS

1	Acknowledgments dedication	i 1
2	Prologue	Pg #iv
3	pictures	Pg #v1-55
4	psalms	Pg #56-107
5	Epilogue	Pg #108
6	Bio	Pg #109

Poems on pictures

A GODLY HUSBAND

Prophet, Priest and a King
The Word of God he does bring
Protects and serves from a pure heart
Being a provider is but a start

He is the image and glory of the Lord
Fearlessly wielding the two edged sword
A strong, bold and powerful life
He'll gladly lay it down for his wife

Love and compassion from whom does flow
To him his wife will gladly go
A strong bridge over the pressures of life
He'll be blessed with a godly wife.

A GODLY WIFE

Virtuous and compassionate full of love
She is God's gift sent from above
To this woman I shall impart
Wisdom and knowledge to fill her heart

The fear of the Lord makes her just
In her, her husband does trust
To this woman I shall say
Receive my anointing this very day

I shall guide you through your life
Receive my anointing dear Godly wife
Integrity and honor are yours to stay
You shall be blessed day by day.

Michalina

A SPIRITUAL MAN

A spiritual man upright and true
Integrity and love thru and thru
Spiritual pride is not his lot
The grace of God he has sought

A spiritual man quite contagious
Against him the enemy rages
Victories are known through the land
In the power of God he must stand

A spiritual man faithful and true
With him no days are blue
A priest and king he shall be
When Jesus comes for you and me.

THE BLOOD

Standing on the edge of the universe
Proclaiming the Word, but not in verse
Standing tall and strong
Proclaiming words that weren't wrong

Bold and confident I have said
His precious blood has been shed
There I stand where all could see
Proclaiming the blood for eternity

Of His blood I do not plead
Boldness and confidence is what I read
Proclamation of that great name
The powerful blood I will PROCLAIM!!!!

CHILDREN

Wide eyed and innocent of all wrong
Sit the children of this psalm
Confident, trusting, willing to share
The love they experience there

Through these doors my children come
To learn the integrity of my Son
The teachers have quite the task
To answer questions the pupils ask

Love, kindness and righteousness they yearn
Please help my children to learn
Teachers walk upright, do your part
To give the children a righteous start.

COMPANIONS

When we are among friends
The anointing He does send
To keep our thoughts on high
For our praises to ascend to the sky

We are a cheerful joyous lot
The grace of God we have sought
Let us encourage and strengthen
each other
There's a friend who sticks closer
than a brother

Red, white, yellow and blue
Will we be friends quite true?
Looking to the others best
Let's pursue the Word with zest.

DAUGHTER OF THE LORD

To this young child I shall say
Rejoice, rejoice, coming is a better day
Strength and honor I shall impart
To my daughter of a gentle heart

My love extends with resurrection life
Walk in love not in strife
To my daughter I shall say
Search my heart, continue to pray

To the daughter of my grace
I behold your lovely face
I rejoice because your mine
To you my love will forever shine.

DEVIL'S DEMISE

The anointing is flowing
The gifts are growing
The devil is in fear
Because his end is near

When the devil roars in strife
Know for sure he's at the end of his life
Though he connives and does try
Know for sure his attempts will die

Victory is yours for sure
Because of a heart that's pure
Jesus Christ the King on high
Has destroyed the enemy, it's time for him to die

THE ENCOURAGER

Who is this one who brings encouragement,
Obviously one whom heaven has sent
She reaches out when others are down
imparting hope and smiles
in the place of a frown

Who is this one from whom strength flows
On her my anointing continually grows
Bringing joy and peace to all her peers,
She reaches out to wipe their tears

To this child I shall say,
My peace on you shall continually stay
To the one who looks to others best,
Enter thou into my Holy rest.

FAITHFULNESS

I will exalt my only hope
Through your Word I can cope
When life is futile, full of disaster
I shall jump, shout, be filled with
laughter

When my world comes crashing down
I'll sing and dance with no frown
Because of kindness, grace, and love
I shall praise you who is above

A new day is dawning I shall see
Your Word will guide through eternity
In song and dance I have praised
On that third day you were raised

Praise and thanks I stand strong
Because to whom I do belong
You are my hope, mighty king
I will praise you in everything.

FEAR NOT

Fear not, fear not, fear not
I am the salvation you have sought
To deliver you by the power of my blood
The enemy may roar but he's no flood

Through the power of my name
To you salvation has already came
Fear not, fear not, fear not!
My blood your salvation has bought

Fear not! Look to the king on high
Let your praises ascend to the sky
Resurrection power on the way
To deliver from harm every day.

GOD OF COMFORT

My Savior and hope of whom I'll sing
Guides and comforts in everything
To my soul he does impart
His mighty peace to settle my heart

When all the world roars with strife
His great love brings me life
From the cross come blessings more
The chastisement for our peace He has bore

When confusion turns my head
of His Word I have read
Quiet and confidence is my part
Peace and comfort does fill my heart.

THE GIVER

*The giver is one who knows my heart
Giving of themselves is a righteous start
Fulfilling the conditions they have heard
Reaping the promises of My Word*

*The rut of poverty they shall not see
Their giving will excel throughout eternity
Of My ways they have heard
Reaping the promises of My Word*

*The giver is somebody who touches my heart
Tithes and offerings is only a start
The love of God they have heard
Reaping the promises of My Word.*

GOD IN THE HIGHEST

Praise be to God from whom all blessings flow
With love and worship, to Him I shall go
He is my fortress and strong tower
My Jesus comes with resurrection power

He is the light and joy of life
Keeping me from harm and all strife
He is my soon coming King
Bringing joy and causing all to sing

He is the one who looks to my best
Giving joy, peace and eternal rest
Of all the things that come my way
I'll look forward to resurrection day.

GOD'S BEST

*You are worth more than you know
Study my Word, continue to grow
Be strong, you're a child of the king
Success and honor in everything*

*Your destiny brings ultimate success
Don't say no, just say yes
Full of life you shall be
When in faith you look to me*

*Excitement and power, the fruit of life
Wisdom and honor, the absence of strife
Grace and wonders, child of the King
You are blessed in everything.*

© Alex Racanelli Photography

GRACE

Amazing grace how sweet the sounds
Because of love that knows no bounds
I was lost in sin and undone
Redeemed through the cross of your only Son

Grace came with blessings by the score
Jesus stands knocking at our heart's door
Will I let the righteous one in?
To save and redeem from the power of sin

Hosanna in the highest, Holy, Holy one
I receive you in my heart, Jesus the Son
Because of grace you were raised
Forever now to be praised.

HEALING

I was bruised for your iniquities
Look to me not your remedies
I am the Lord of all your health
Healing breaks forth in overflowing wealth

I am the healer, great is my supply
Look to me, you shall not die
I was wounded for your transgressions
Your healing comes in many successions

By my stripes you have been healed
With my Spirit you were sealed
Use my name, be so quick
I've delivered you, don't be sick.

OPEN HEAVENS

Open heavens are the things you want
Closed heavens are the devil's taunts
When you release those rivers of water
The devil shall flee because of his slaughter

When in intercessory prayer you fight
Beams and shafts of Holy light
Shall penetrate the blanket of dark
Be fervent because there is a great spark

Be strong, faithful and ready to fight
Because you shall see darkness blasted by light
Faith and confident you shall stand
Glorious victory o so grand!

HELPER

The helper is one to whom you must run
When battles are to be won
Imparting bravery, strength and might
Be valiant, be brave, continue to fight

When in weakness, lost or confused
Resist the enemy, don't be abused
The helper is there to lend a hand
In the power of God you shall stand

Who is this helper? What's His name?
The Holy Spirit, the one and the same
The enemy comes bringing strife
Run to the author of all life

He is your help in time of need
Of His instruction do take heed
Author of life to one and all
Bless God! I'm redeemed from the fall.

HELPER

The helper is one to whom you must run
When battles are to be won
Imparting bravery, strength and might
Be valiant, be brave, continue to fight

When in weakness, bruised and abused
Resist the enemy, don't be abused
The helper is there to lend a hand
In the power of God you shall stand

Who is this helper? What's His name?
The Holy Spirit, His one and the same
The enemy comes bringing strife
Run to the author of all life

He is your help in time of need
Of His instruction do take heed
Author of life to one and all
Bless God, I'm redeemed from the fall.

HOME

Alone and majestic it does stand
Strong arms reaching out so grand
Bringing protection to those below
An umbrella from the deep snow

Standing upright in an open field
To others its fruit to yield
What is this sight I see
But a lonely spruce tree

Many look and see no good
Just a big old chunk of wood
But to the animals which do roam
This tree is called home

There is a moral to this psalm
Don't condemn just be calm
Others may not measure up
But whose to say what's their cup

HUSBAND TO HIS WIFE

To the one who's a gift from above
You are beautiful in whom I find love
Please be patient with me every day
I sometimes get confused and lose my way

Don't be angry or full of strife
I too am filled with resurrection life
Please be an encourager when my days are blue
Because truly, I do love you

I am being changed, God's tugging at my heart
Life's a challenge, I want to do my part
Hold me tight, I need your love
Cut me slack, don't push or shove

I am a man who's sensitive at heart
But my feelings I don't easily impart
Soon I will raise up in the right hour
Flowing with God's resurrection power.

JESUS

Jesus Christ, the Lord my rock
In His presence I shall walk
Glory and strength, full of love
My dear Jesus, sent from above

Strength and honor He will impart
To everyone who is pure of heart
Kindness radiates from His eyes
A man of integrity, with no lies

The Lord my Savior, full of grace
Gentleness shines from His face
Love extends and knows no bound
A greater God, who has found?

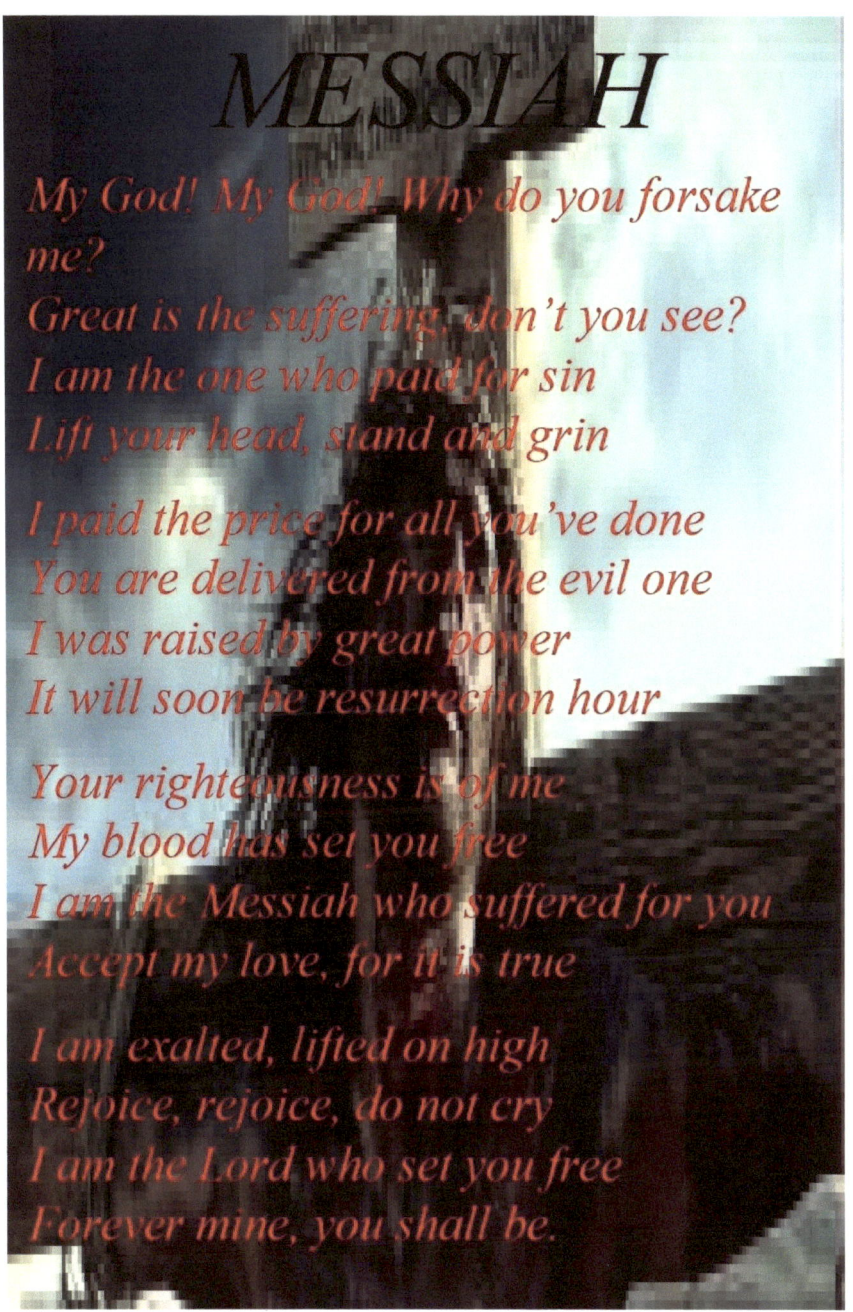

MESSIAH

My God! My God! Why do you forsake me?
Great is the suffering, don't you see?
I am the one who paid for sin
Lift your head, stand and grin

I paid the price for all you've done
You are delivered from the evil one
I was raised by great power
It will soon be resurrection hour

Your righteousness is of me
My blood has set you free
I am the Messiah who suffered for you
Accept my love, for it is true

I am exalted, lifted on high
Rejoice, rejoice, do not cry
I am the Lord who set you free
Forever mine, you shall be.

MOTHER

Patient and gentle she does stand
Kindness and grace are her's to command
Peace and contentment with no strife
She lives a quiet and Godly life

In wisdom and knowledge she does grow
With gentle words she helps us to know
The guidance to fulfill our lives part
Love comes from the depths of her heart

Power and strength to radiate
Disobedience she does hate
A gift of heaven she is from
I'll look forward to calling her... MOM.

MOTHER

Patient and gentle she does stand
Kindness and grace are her's to command
Peace and contentment with no strife
She lives a quiet and Godly life

In wisdom and knowledge she does grow
With gentle words she helps us to know
The guidance to fulfill our lives part
Love comes from the depths of her heart

Power and strength to radiate
Disobedience she does hate
A gift of heaven she is from
I'll look forward to calling her... MOM.

NATURE

The birds, flowers and trees do sing
Rejoicing in the Lord their melodies ring
Watching the sun about half past five
When all of a sudden the breeze was alive

As the breeze continued on bye
The name of Jesus was exalted on high
As the anointing began to flow
A new revelation for me to know

Then one day while reading the Word
All excited over the phrase I heard
Sun, moon, and stars of light
Praise His name this very night.

PREACHER

To be a preacher of the Word
Blessing the many who have heard
To skillfully wield the two edged sword
Being a vessel of the Lord

Son of man hear my Word
Bless the many who have heard
Store My sayings in your heart
Deliver My Word that's your part

Son of man, this I say
Study the Word every day
Go to the people, tell them so
Whether they say yes, whether they say no

Blessed is the Lord from His place
Being a preacher is only through grace
I'll skillfully preach the mighty Word
Blessing the many who have heard

RESURRECTION DAY

Once upon a time, long, long ago
My Spirit broke forth to show
The mighty power of the Lord
To bring judgment like a sword

From this time I have gone
To bring forth grace with a song
This very day you shall see
Glorious power with victory

When my power starts to flood
Honor my presence through the blood
When I come this very night
Resurrection power giving sight

Glorious power you shall see
Coming forth to victory
To my church I shall say
You have entered a special day

Be bold, strong and diligent
My resurrection power I have sent
To my church I shall say
Get ready! It's Resurrection Day!!

RESURRECTION DAY

Once upon a time, long, long ago
My Spirit broke forth to show
The mighty power of the Lord
To bring judgment like a sword

From this time I have gone
To bring forth grace with a song
This very day you shall see
Glorious power with victory

When my power starts to flood
Honor my presence through the blood
When I come this very night
Resurrection power giving sight

Glorious power you shall see
Coming forth to victory
To my church I shall say
You have entered a special day

Be bold, strong and diligent
My resurrection power I have sent
To my church I shall say
Get ready! It's Resurrection Day!!

THE SHEPHERD

O my King! To you I'll sing
You have blessed in everything
All around, the shadow of death
I'm delivered by your breath

The breath of life fills my heart
On the paths of righteousness I shall start
Of the evil I will not fear
Because of your presence O so near

Power and authority I do know
My enemy runs, watch him go
Boldness and mercy all of my life
Quiet times with no strife

I'll live in the house of the Lord
Protected by your two edged sword
Your testimony and covenant I shall keep
Because your anointing guides my feet.

SUCCESS

You are my rock and fortress
The Lord of all my success
Spirit, soul, and body, you want my best
Your Word, I'll pursue with zest

When pressure tries my faith
I'll walk in the Word of Grace
You will never leave me in a spot
I'll not allow my harvest to rot

I am the Lord of all your success
In righteous ways you shall dress
Honor, integrity and pureness of heart
Covenant power for a successful start.

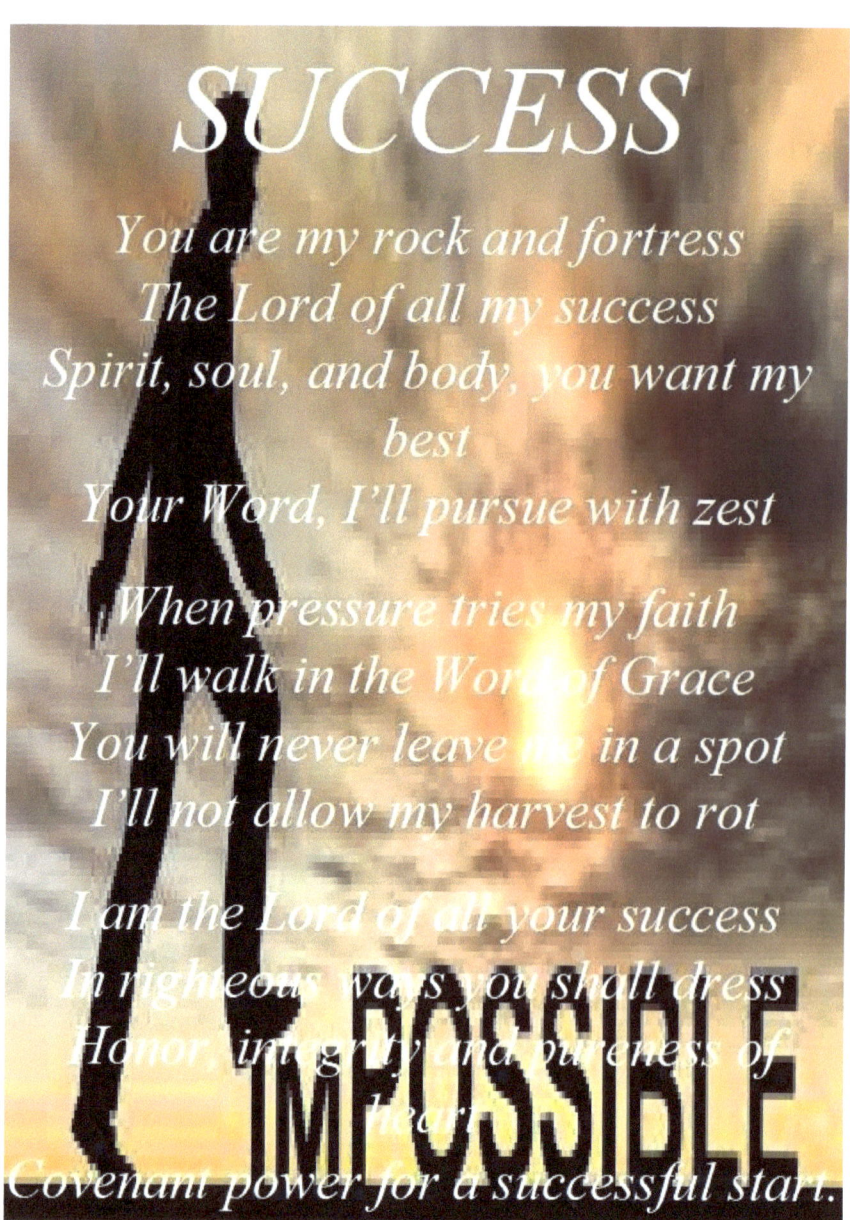

SUCCESS

You are my rock and fortress
The Lord of all my success
Spirit, soul, and body, you want my best
Your Word, I'll pursue with zest

When pressure tries my faith
I'll walk in the Word of Grace
You will never leave me in a spot
I'll not allow my harvest to rot

I am the Lord of all your success
In righteous ways you shall dress
Honor, integrity and pureness of heart
Covenant power for a successful start.

THE SUPPER OF THE LAMB

A banqueting table, the supper of the Lord
A place of honor or judgment with the sword
Blessing and glory and honor and power
Or judgment in that final hour

Blessings on the marriage supper of the Lamb
A place of honor for the worshippers of the " I Am "
The birds that fly in the midst of heaven
Dine on meat with no leaven

Rejoice, the marriage of the Lamb
Servants arrayed in the linen of the " I Am "
Out of His mouth goes a sharp sword
To strike the ungodly horde

The supper of the Lamb! Let us rejoice
A great choir all of one voice
Hide us from the wrath of the Lamb
We are enemies of the " I Am "

The question is to you my friends
Which shall it be to send
A child of the great " I Am "
Or an enemy of the Lamb?

THE SUPPER OF THE LAMB

A banqueting table, the supper of the Lord
A place of honor or judgment with the sword
Blessing and glory and honor and power
Or judgment in that final hour

Blessings at the marriage supper of the Lamb
A place of honor for the worshippers of the " I Am "
The birds that fly in the midst of heaven
Dine on meat with no leaven

Rejoice, the marriage of the Lamb
Servants arrayed in the linen of the " I Am "
Out of His mouth goes a sharp sword
To strike the ungodly horde

The supper of the Lamb! Let us rejoice
A great choir all of one voice
Hide us from the wrath of the Lamb
We are enemies of the " I Am "

The question is to you my friends
Which stanza to you to send
A child of the great " I Am "
Or an enemy of the Lamb?

TEARS ON A SHOULDER

The tears on your shoulder are there for a reason
The person who left them there was expressing emotion
Joy or sorrow, who can say,
What the emotion of the day

The real question I have to ask
The shoulder cried on is it a task
Many will be bothered by the tear
The color on my sweater is smeared

Are you full of love fulfilling your part?
Your shoulder, a place for others to lay their heart
Satisfaction will be yours I can say
When on your shoulder hearts can lay

William Hatfield

TEARS ON A SHOULDER

The tears on your shoulder are there for a reason
The person who left them there was expressing emotion
Joy or sorrow, who can say,
What the emotion of the day

The real question I have to ask
The shoulder cried on is it a task
Many will be bothered by the tear
The color on my sweater is smeared

Are you full of love fulfilling your part?
Your shoulder, a place for others to lay their heart
Satisfaction will be yours I can say
When on your shoulder hearts can lay

William Hatfield

THE NAME

The name which is above every name
Power and might found in the same
Love and compassion from whom does flow
This precious name we must know

At the sound of the name from above
Every knee shall bow, reaching for love
Of His Lordship they shall confess
Love of that name saints do express

To the exalted name from above
A heart of compassion filled with love
Who is this majestic mighty one?
Jesus Christ, the omnipotent Holy Son.

THE NAME

The name which is above every name
Power and might found in the same
Love and compassion from whom does flow
This precious name we must know

At the sound of the name from above
Every knee shall bow, reaching for love
Of His Lordship they shall confess
Love of that name saints do express

To the exalted name from above
A heart of compassion filled with love
Who is this majestic mighty one?
Jesus Christ, the omnipotent Holy Son.

THE PRESENCE

With pureness of heart I shall stand
In your presence O so grand
Majestic angels all around
Rejoicing! A glorious sound

I shall stand before you on that day
Until then I will continue to pray
Your presence, I have sought
With your blood I was bought

I am a child of the most high
In your presence, my tears you shall dry
In your presence I shall stand
Rejoicing in song O so grand.

THE PRESENCE

With pureness of heart I shall stand
In your presence O so grand
Majestic angels all around
Rejoicing! A glorious sound

I shall stand before you on that day
Until then I will continue to pray
Your presence, I have sought
With your blood I was bought

I am a child of the most high
In your presence, my tears you shall dry
In your presence I shall stand
Rejoicing in song O so grand.

THE RIDER

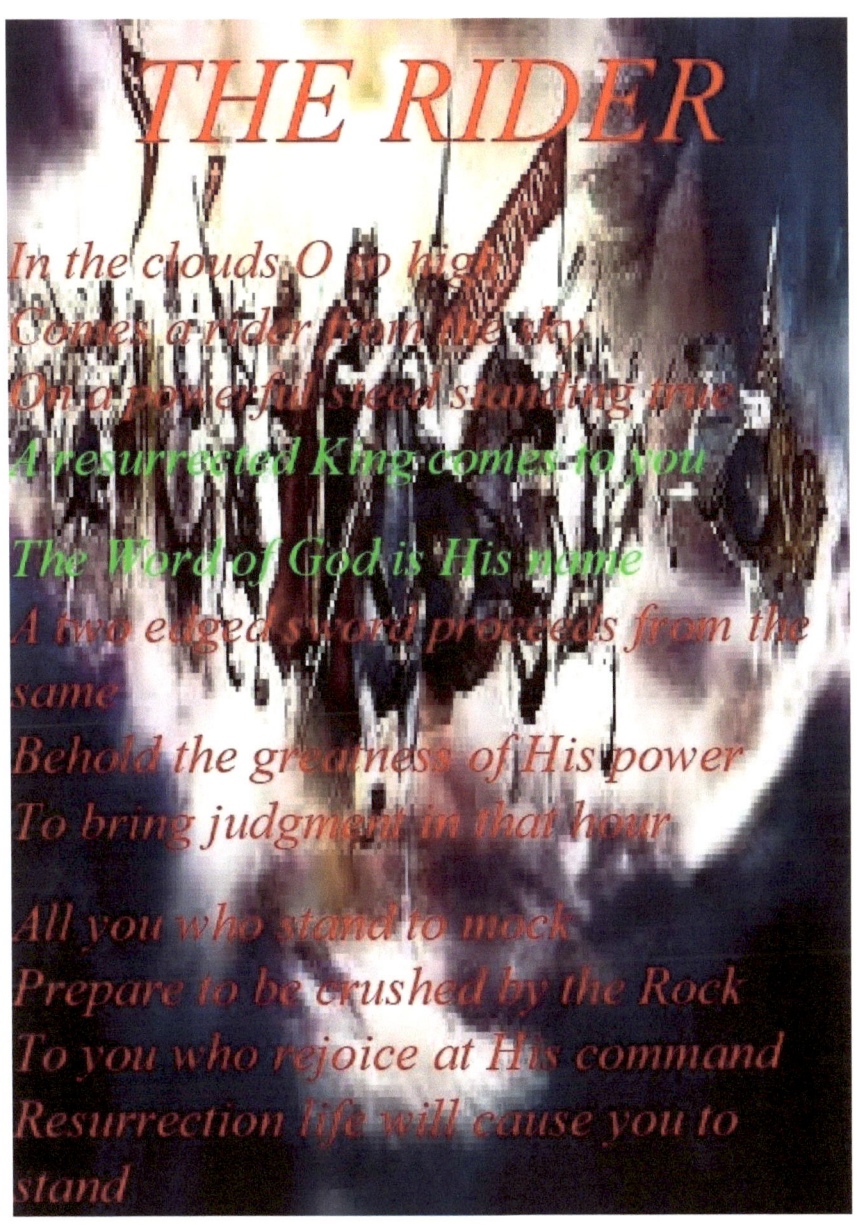

In the clouds, O so high,
Comes a rider from the sky,
On a powerful steed standing true
A resurrected King comes to you

The Word of God is His name
A two edged sword proceeds from the same
Behold the greatness of His power
To bring judgment in that hour

All you who stand to mock
Prepare to be crushed by the Rock
To you who rejoice at His command
Resurrection life will cause you to stand

THE RIDER

In the clouds O so high
Comes a rider from the sky
On a powerful steed standing true
A resurrected King comes to you

The Word of God is His name
A two edged sword proceeds from the same
Behold the greatness of His power
To bring judgment in that hour

All you who stand to mock
Prepare to be crushed by the Rock
To you who rejoice at His command
Resurrection life will cause you to stand

SOULWINNER

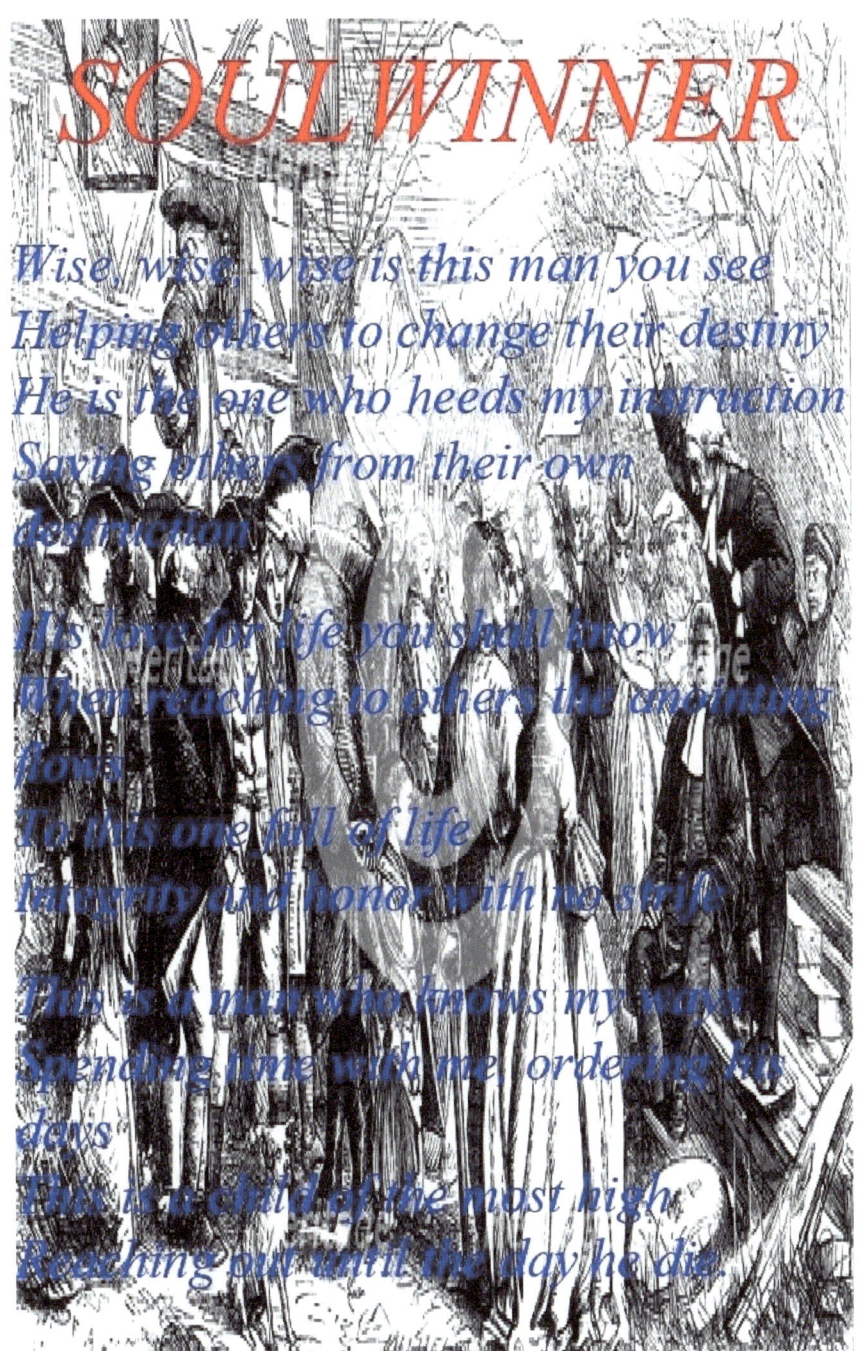

Wise, wise, wise is this man you see
Helping others to change their destiny
He is the one who heeds my instruction
Saving others from their own destruction
His love for life you shall know
When reaching to others the anointing flows
To this one full of life
Integrity and honor with no strife
This is a man who knows my ways
Spending time with me, ordering his days
This is a child of the most high
Reaching out until the day he dies

SOULWINNER

Wise, wise, wise is this man you see
Helping others to change their destiny
He is the one who heeds my instruction
Saving others from their own destruction

His love for life you shall know
When reaching to others the anointing flows
To this one full of life
Integrity and honor with no strife

This is a man who knows my ways
Spending time with me, ordering his days
This is a child of the most high
Reaching out until the day he die.

THE WORD

The Word is precious to me
Upholding and strengthening for eternity
The Word brings healing this I know
In times of trouble to the Word I go

Powerful, living, sharp and quick
The Word delivers those that are sick
In the Word I find sustenance
Guiding and directing to repentance

I'm in love with the righteous Word
Inspiring faith in all who heard
The Father, the Word, the Holy One
Set free to worship the righteous Son.

THE WORD

*The Word is precious to me
Upholding and strengthening for
eternity
The Word brings healing this I know
In times of trouble to the Word I go*

*Powerful, living, sharp and quick
The Word delivers those that are
sick
In the Word I find sustenance
Guiding and directing to repentance*

*I'm in love with the righteous Word
Inspiring faith in all who heard
The Father, the Word, the Holy One
Set free to worship the righteous
Son.*

THRONEROOM

A voice majestically does sound
Thunder and lightning's all around
Twenty four elders clothed in white
Seven lamps burning bright

The living creatures O what a sight
Crying Holy, Holy day and night
Thousands of angels all around
All together with one sound

Worthy, worthy is the Lamb
Power and Honor from the I am
Blessing and honor, glory and power
To the Lamb in that grand hour

THRONEROOM

A voice majestically does sound
Thunder and lightning's all around
Twenty four elders clothed in white
Seven lamps burning bright

The living creatures O what a sight
Crying Holy, Holy day and night
Thousands of angels all around
All together with one sound

Worthy, worthy is the Lamb
Power and Honor from the I am
Blessing and honor, glory and power
To the Lamb in that grand hour

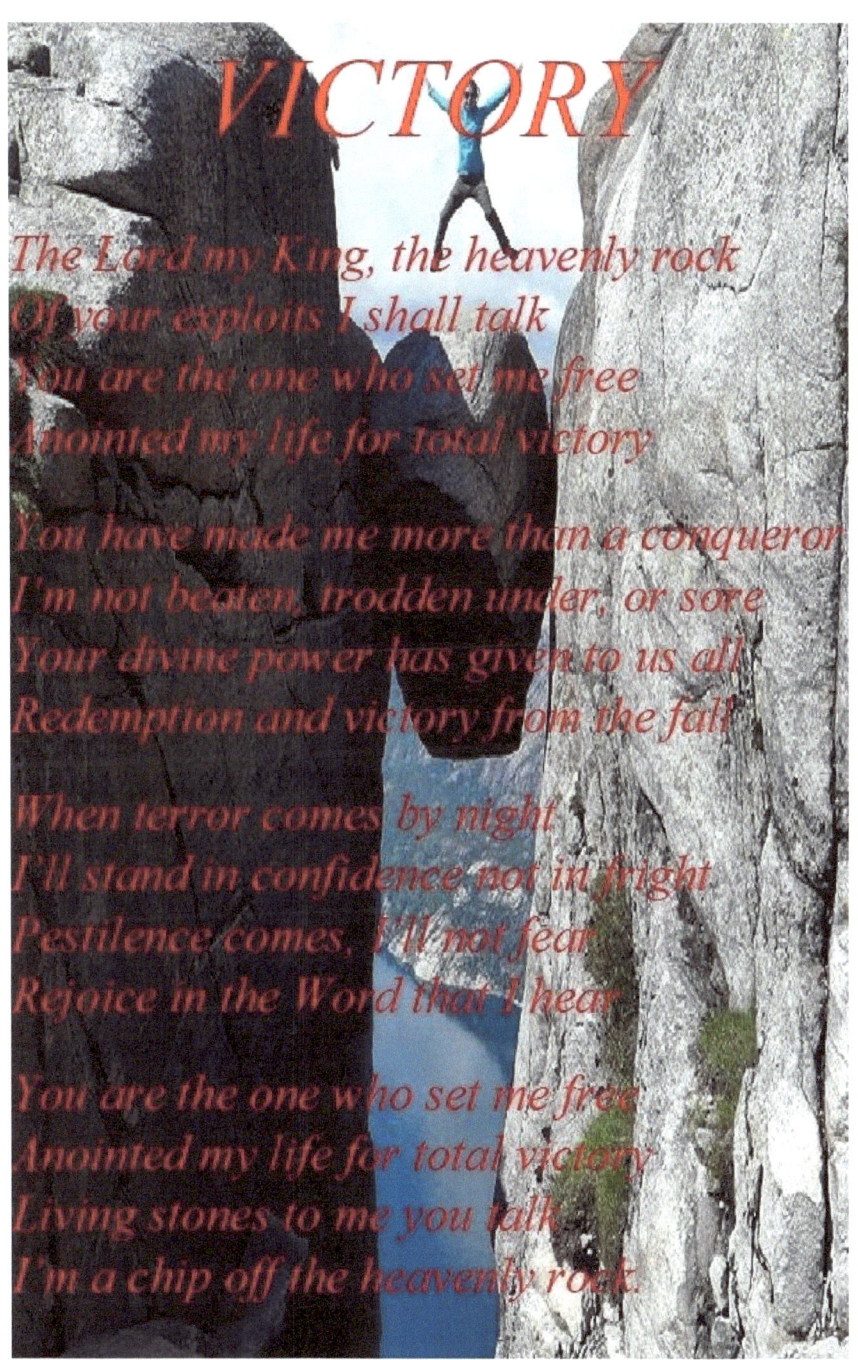

VICTORY

The Lord my King, the heavenly rock
Of your exploits I shall talk
You are the one who set me free
Anointed my life for total victory

You have made me more than a conqueror
I'm not beaten, trodden under, or sore
Your divine power has given to us all
Redemption and victory from the fall

When terror comes by night
I'll stand in confidence not in fright
Pestilence comes, I'll not fear
Rejoice in the Word that I hear

You are the one who set me free
Anointed my life for total victory
Living stones to me you talk
I'm a chip off the heavenly rock.

VICTORY

The Lord my King, the heavenly rock
Of your exploits I shall talk
You are the one who set me free
Anointed my life for total victory

You have made me more than a conqueror
I'm not beaten, trodden under, or sore
Your divine power has given to us all
Redemption and victory from the fall

When terror comes by night
I'll stand in confidence not in fright
Pestilence comes, I'll not fear
Rejoice in the Word that I hear

You are the one who set me free
Anointed my life for total victory
Living stones to me you talk
I'm a chip off the heavenly rock.

WAIT UPON THE LORD

Those who wait upon the Lord
Shall be tempered as a two edged sword
They shall walk and not tire
The anointing of God lifts them higher

They shall run and not pass out
In victory songs they do shout
Honor and integrity are their lot
The grace of God they have sought

They shall mount up with wings as an eagle
Splendorous they soar, O so regal
They shall walk in robes of royal thread
Blessed be the Word I have read.

WARRIOR

A warrior is one who stands to fight
For everything he believes is right
Sin and unrighteousness he will not condone
He will continue to stand, even if alone

The weapons of his warfare he does know
The battle cry has sounded, he is the first to go
Wise and cunning he proceeds to fight
For everything he believes to be right

This one is special don't you see
Helping others to attain liberty
Humble and honorable, quite so real
Resurrection power when he kneels

When a battle rages here or there
He shall proceed through Word and prayer
The Lord is raising an army you see
To march to war on their knees.

WARRIOR

A warrior is one who stands to fight
For everything he believes is right
Sin and unrighteousness he will not condone
He will continue to stand, even if alone

The weapons of his warfare he does know
The battle cry has sounded, he is the first to go
Wise and cunning he proceeds to fight
For everything he believes to be right

This one is special don't you see
Helping others to attain liberty
Humble and honorable, quite so real
Resurrection power when he kneels

When a battle rages here or there
He shall proceed through Word and prayer
The Lord is raising an army you see
To march to war on their knees.

CRASHING DOWN

WHEN THE WORLD COMES CRASHING DOWN

WHY DO I PROCEED WITH A FROWN

OUTWARD APPERANCES RUN ME AROUND

HOW MANY GOD'S ARE REALLY SOUND

WHEN TIMES ARE CHALLENGING AND VERY ROUGH

WHOM DO I LOOK TO I HAVE HAD ENOUGH

JESUS CHRIST MY KING ON HIGH

TO YOU I LOOK WIPE THE TEAR DRY

BRING ABOUT EVERLASTING JOY

MY EMOTIONS ARE NOT A TOY

WHEN PEOPLE TO ME TRY TO SCAM

REVEAL TO THEM WHO IS THE GREAT I AM

CRASHING DOWN

WHEN THE WORLD COMES CRASHING DOWN

WHY DO I PROCEED WITH A FROWN

OUTWARD APPERANCES RUN ME AROUND

HOW MANY GOD'S ARE REALLY SOUND

`WHEN TIMES ARE CHALLENGING AND VERY ROUGH

WHOM DO I LOOK TO I HAVE HAD ENOUGH

JESUS CHRIST MY KING ON HIGH

TO YOU I LOOK WIPE THE TEAR DRY

BRING ABOUT EVERLASTING JOY

MY EMOTIONS ARE NOT A TOY

WHEN PEOPLE TO ME TRY TO SCAM

REVEAL TO THEM WHO IS THE GREAT I AM

CRASHING DOWN

WHEN THE WORLD COMES CRASHING DOWN

WHY DO I PROCEED WITH A FROWN

OUTWARD APPERANCES RUN ME AROUND

HOW MANY GOD'S ARE REALLY SOUND

`WHEN TIMES ARE CHALLENGING AND VERY ROUGH

WHOM DO I LOOK TO I HAVE HAD ENOUGH

JESUS CHRIST MY KING ON HIGH

TO YOU I LOOK WIPE THE TEAR DRY

BRING ABOUT EVERLASTING JOY

MY EMOTIONS ARE NOT A TOY

WHEN PEOPLE TO ME TRY TO SCAM

REVEAL TO THEM WHO IS THE GREAT I AM

WARRIOR

A warrior is one who stands to fight

For everything he believes is right

Sin and unrighteousness he will not condone

He will continue to stand, even if alone

The weapons of his warfare he does know

The battle cry has sounded, he is the first to go

Wise and cunning he proceeds to fight

For everything he believes to be right

This one is special don't you see

Helping others to attain liberty

Humble and honorable, quite so real

Resurrection power when he kneels

When a battle rages here or there

He shall proceed through Word and prayer

The Lord is raising an army you see

To march to war on their knees.

VICTORY

The Lord my King, the heavenly rock

Of your exploits I shall talk

You are the one who set me free

Anointed my life for total victory

You have made me more than a conqueror

I'm not beaten, trodden under, or sore

Your divine power has given to us all

Redemption and victory from the fall

When terror comes by night

I'll stand in confidence not in fright

Pestilence comes, I'll not fear

Rejoice in the Word that I hear

You are the one who set me free

Anointed my life for total victory

Living stones to me you talk

I'm a chip off the heavenly rock.

THRONEROOM

A voice majestically does sound

Thunder and lightning's all around

Twenty four elders clothed in white

Seven lamps burning bright

The living creatures O what a sight

Crying Holy, Holy day and night

Thousands of angels all around

All together with one sound

Worthy, worthy is the Lamb

Power and Honor from the I am

Blessing and honor, glory and power

To the Lamb in that grand hour

THE BLOOD

Standing on the edge of the universe

Proclaiming the Word, but not in verse

Standing tall and strong

Proclaiming words that weren't wrong

Bold and confident I have said

His precious blood has been shed

There I stand where all could see

Proclaiming the blood for eternity

Of His blood I do not plead

Boldness and confidence is what I read

Proclamation of that great name

The powerful blood I will PROCLAIM!!!!

THE WORD

The Word is precious to me

Upholding and strengthening for eternity

The Word brings healing this I know

In times of trouble to the Word I go

Powerful, living, sharp and quick

The Word delivers those that are sick

In the Word I find sustenance

Guiding and directing to repentance

I'm in love with the righteous Word

Inspiring faith in all who heard

The Father, the Word, the Holy One

Set free to worship the righteous Son.

SOULWINNER

Wise, wise, wise is this man you see

Helping others to change their destiny

He is the one who heeds my instruction

Saving others from their own destruction

His love for life you shall know

When reaching to others the anointing flows

To this one full of life

Integrity and honor with no strife

This is a man who knows my ways

Spending time with me, ordering his days

This is a child of the most high

Reaching out until the day he die.

THE SHEPHERD

O my King! To you I'll sing

You have blessed in everything

All around, the shadow of death

I'm delivered by your breath

The breath of life fills my heart

On the paths of righteousness I shall start

Of the evil I will not fear

Because of your presence O so near

Power and authority I do know

My enemy runs, watch him go

Boldness and mercy all of my life

Quiet times with no strife

I'll live in the house of the Lord

Protected by your two edged sword

Your testimony and covenant I shall keep

Because your anointing guides my feet.

THE PRESENCE

With pureness of heart I shall stand

In your presence O so grand

Majestic angels all around

Rejoicing! A glorious sound

I shall stand before you on that day

Until then I will continue to pray

Your presence, I have sought

With your blood I was bought

I am a child of the most high

In your presence, my tears you shall dry

In your presence I shall stand

Rejoicing in song O so grand.

THE NAME

The name which is above every name

Power and might found in the same

Love and compassion from whom does flow

This precious name we must know

At the sound of the name from above

Every knee shall bow, reaching for love

Of His Lordship they shall confess

Love of that name saints do express

To the exalted name from above

A heart of compassion filled with love

Who is this majestic mighty one?

Jesus Christ, the omnipotent Holy Son.

TEARS ON A SHOULDER

The tears on your shoulder are there for a reason

the person who left them there was expressing emotion

joy or sorrow, who can say

what the emotion of the day

The real question I have to ask

the shoulder cried on is it a task

many will be bothered by the tear

the color on my sweater is smeared

are you full of love fulfilling your part

your shoulder, a place for others to lay their heart

satisfaction will be yours I can say

when on your shoulder hearts can lay

THE SUPPER OF THE LAMB

A banqueting table, the supper of the Lord

A place of honor or judgment with the sword

Blessing and glory and honor and power

Or judgment in that final hour

Blessings at the marriage supper of the Lamb

A place of honor for the worshippers of the " I Am "

The birds that fly in the midst of heaven

Dine on meat with no leaven

Rejoice, the marriage of the Lamb

Servants arrayed in the linen of the " I Am "

Out of His mouth goes a sharp sword

To strike the ungodly horde

The supper of the Lamb! Let us rejoice

A great choir all of one voice

Hide us from the wrath of the Lamb

We are enemies of the " I Am "

The question is to you my friends

Which stanza to you to send

A child of the great " I Am "

Or an enemy of the Lamb?

SUCCESS

You are my rock and fortress

The Lord of all my success

Spirit, soul, and body, you want my best

Your Word, I'll pursue with zest

When pressure tries my faith

I'll walk in the Word of Grace

You will never leave me in a spot

I'll not allow my harvest to rot

I am the Lord of all your success

In righteous ways you shall dress

Honor, integrity and pureness of heart

Covenant power for a successful start.

THE RIDER

In the clouds O so high

Comes a rider from the sky

On a powerful steed standing true

A resurrected King comes to you

The Word of God is His name

A two edged sword proceeds from the same

Behold the greatness of His power

To bring judgment in that hour

All you who stand to mock

Prepare to be crushed by the Rock

To you who rejoice at His command

Resurrection life will cause you to stand

RESURRECTION DAY

Once upon a time, long, long ago

My Spirit broke forth to show

The mighty power of the Lord

To bring judgment like a sword

From this time I have gone

To bring forth grace with a song

This very day you shall see

Glorious power with victory

When my power starts to flood

Honor my presence through the blood

When I come this very night

Resurrection power giving sight

Glorious power you shall see

Coming forth to victory

To my church I shall say

You have entered a special day

Be bold, strong and diligent

My resurrection power I have sent

To my church I shall say

Get ready! It's Resurrection Day!!

PREACHER

To be a preacher of the Word

Blessing the many who have heard

To skillfully wield the two edged sword

Being a vessel of the Lord

Son of man hear my Word

Bless the many who have heard

Store My sayings in your heart

Deliver My Word that's your part

Son of man, this I say

Study the Word every day

Go to the people, tell them so

Whether they say yes, whether they say no

Blessed is the Lord from His place

Being a preacher is only through grace

I'll skillfully preach the mighty Word

Blessing the many who have heard.

NATURE

The birds, flowers and trees do sing

Rejoicing in the Lord their melodies ring

Watching the sun about half past five

When all of a sudden the breeze was alive

As the breeze continued on bye

The name of Jesus was exalted on high

As the anointing began to flow

A new revelation for me to know

Then one day while reading the Word

All excited over the phrase I heard

Sun, moon and stars of light

Praise His name this very night.

MOTHER

Patient and gentle she does stand

Kindness and grace are hers to command

Peace and contentment with no strife

She lives a quiet and Godly life

In wisdom and knowledge she does grow

With gentle words she helps us to know

The guidance to fulfill our lives part

Love comes from the depths of her heart

Power and strength to radiate

Disobedience she does hate

A gift of heaven she is from

I'll look forward to calling her... MOM.

MESSIAH

My God! My God! Why do you forsake me?

Great is the suffering, don't you see?

I am the one who paid for sin

Lift your head, stand and grin

I paid the price for all you've done

You are delivered from the evil one

I was raised by great power

It will soon be resurrection hour

Your righteousness is of me

My blood has set you free

I am the Messiah who suffered for you

Accept my love, for it is true

I am exalted, lifted on high

Rejoice, rejoice, do not cry

I am the Lord who set you free

Forever mine, you shall be.

JESUS

Jesus Christ, the Lord my rock

In His presence I shall walk

Glory and strength, full of love

My dear Jesus, sent from above

Strength and honor He will impart

To everyone who is pure of heart

Kindness radiates from His eyes

A man of integrity, with no lies

The Lord my Savior, full of grace

Gentleness shines from His face

Love extends and knows no bound

A greater God, who has found?

HUSBAND TO HIS WIFE

To the one who's a gift from above

You are beautiful in whom I find love

Please be patient with me every day

I sometimes get confused and lose my way

Don't be angry or full of strife

I too am filled with resurrection life

Please be an encourager when my days are blue

Because truly, I do love you

I am being changed, God's tugging at my heart

Life's a challenge, I want to do my part

Hold me tight, I need your love

Cut me slack, don't push or shove

I am a man who's sensitive at heart

But my feelings I don't easily impart

Soon I will raise up in the right hour

Flowing with God's resurrection power.

HOME

Alone and majestic it does stand

Strong arms reaching out so grand

Bringing protection to those below

An umbrella from the deep snow

Standing upright in an open field

To others its fruit to yield

What is this sight I see

But a lonely spruce tree

Many look and see no good

Just a big old chunk of wood

But to the animals which do roam

This tree is called home

There is a moral to this psalm

Don't condemn just be calm

Others may not measure up

But who's to say what's their cup

HELPER

The helper is one to whom you must run

When battles are to be won

Imparting bravery, strength and might

Be valiant, be brave, continue to fight

When in weakness, lost or confused

Resist the enemy, don't be abused

The helper is there to lend a hand

In the power of God you shall stand

Who is this helper? What's His name?

The Holy Spirit, the one and the same

The enemy comes bringing strife

Run to the author of all life

He is your help in time of need

Of His instruction do take heed

Author of life to one and all

Bless God! I'm redeemed from the fall.

OPEN HEAVENS

Open heavens are the things you want

Closed heavens are the devil's taunts

When you release those rivers of water

The devil shall flee because of his slaughter

When in intercessory prayer you fight

Beams and shafts of Holy light

Shall penetrate the blanket of dark

Be fervent because there is a great spark

Be strong, faithful and ready to fight

Because you shall see darkness blasted by light

Faith and confident you shall stand

Glorious victory o so grand!

HEALING

I was bruised for your iniquities

Look to me not your remedies

I am the Lord of all your health

Healing breaks forth in overflowing wealth

I am the healer, great is my supply

Look to me, you shall not die

I was wounded for your transgressions

Your healing comes in many successions

By my stripes you have been healed

With my Spirit you were sealed

Use my name, be so quick

I've delivered you, don't be sick.

GRACE

Amazing grace how sweet the sounds

Because of love that knows no bounds

I was lost in sin and undone

Redeemed through the cross of your only Son

Grace came with blessings by the score

Jesus stands knocking at our heart's door

Will I let the righteous one in?

To save and redeem from the power of sin

Hosanna in the highest, Holy, Holy one

I receive you in my heart, Jesus the Son

Because of grace you were raised

Forever now to be praised.

GOD'S BEST

You are worth more than you know

Study my Word, continue to grow

Be strong, you're a child of the king

Success and honor in everything

Your destiny brings ultimate success

Don't say no, just say yes

Full of life you shall be

When in faith you look to me

Excitement and power, the fruit of life

Wisdom and honor, the absence of strife

Grace and wonders, child of the King

You are blessed in everything.

GOD OF COMFORT

My Savior and hope of whom I'll sing

Guides and comforts in everything

To my soul he does impart

His mighty peace to settle my heart

When all the world roars with strife

His great love brings me life

From the cross come blessings more

The chastisement for our peace He has bore

When confusion turns my head

of His Word I have read

Quiet and confidence is my part

Peace and comfort does fill my heart.

GOD IN THE HIGHEST

Praise be to God from whom all blessings flow

With love and worship, to Him I shall go

He is my fortress and strong tower

My Jesus comes with resurrection power

He is the light and joy of life

Keeping me from harm and all strife

He is my soon coming King

Bringing joy and causing all to sing

He is the one who looks to my best

Giving joy, peace and eternal rest

Of all the things that come my way

I'll look forward to resurrection day.

THE GIVER

The giver is one who knows my heart

Giving of themselves is a righteous start

Fulfilling the conditions they have heard

Reaping the promises of My Word

The rut of poverty they shall not see

Their giving will excel throughout eternity

Of My ways they have heard

Reaping the promises of My Word

The giver is somebody who touches my heart

Tithes and offerings is only a start

The love of God they have heard

Reaping the promises of My Word.

FEAR NOT

Fear not, fear not, fear not

I am the salvation you have sought

To deliver you by the power of my blood

The enemy may roar but he's no flood

Through the power of my name

To you salvation has already came

Fear not, fear not, fear not!

My blood your salvation has bought

Fear not! Look to the king on high

Let your praises ascend to the sky

Resurrection power on the way

To deliver from harm every day.

FAITHFULNESS

I will exalt my only hope

Through your Word I can cope

When life is futile, full of disaster

I shall jump, shout, be filled with laughter

When my world comes crashing down

I'll sing and dance with no frown

Because of kindness, grace, and love

I shall praise you who is above

A new day is dawning I shall see

Your Word will guide through eternity

In song and dance I have praised

On that third day you were raised

Praise and thanks I stand strong

Because to whom I do belong

You are my hope, mighty king

I will praise you in everything.

THE ENCOURAGER

Who is this one who brings encouragement

Obviously one whom heaven has sent

She reaches out when others are down

imparting hope and smiles

in the place of a frown

Who is this one from whom strength flows

On her my anointing continually grows

Bringing joy and peace to all her peers

She reaches out to wipe their tears

To this child I shall say,

My peace on you shall continually stay

To the one who looks to others best,

Enter thou into my Holy rest.

DEVIL'S DEMISE

The anointing is flowing

The gifts are growing

The devil is in fear

Because his end is near

When the devil roars in strife

Know for sure he's at the end of his life

Though he connives and does try

Know for sure his attempts will die

Victory is yours for sure

Because of a heart that's pure

Jesus Christ the King on high

Has destroyed the enemy, it's time for him to die

DAUGHTER OF THE LORD

To this young child I shall say

Rejoice, rejoice, coming is a better day

Strength and honor I shall impart

To my daughter of a gentle heart

My love extends with resurrection life

Walk in love not in strife

To my daughter I shall say

Search my heart, continue to pray

To the daughter of my grace

I behold your lovely face

I rejoice because your mine

To you my love will forever shine.

COMPANIONS

When we are among friends

The anointing He does send

To keep our thoughts on high

For our praises to ascend to the sky

We are a cheerful joyous lot

The grace of God we have sought

Let us encourage and strengthen each other

There's a friend who sticks closer than a brother

Red, white, yellow and blue

Will we be friends quite true?

Looking to the others best

Let's pursue the Word with zest.

CHILDREN

Wide eyed and innocent of all wrong

Sit the children of this psalm

Confident, trusting, willing to share

The love they experience there

Through these doors my children come

To learn the integrity of my Son

The teachers have quite the task

To answer questions the pupils ask

Love, kindness and righteousness they yearn

Please help my children to learn

Teachers walk upright, do your part

To give the children a righteous start.

THE BLOOD

Standing on the edge of the universe

Proclaiming the Word, but not in verse

Standing tall and strong

Proclaiming words that weren't wrong

Bold and confident I have said

His precious blood has been shed

There I stand where all could see

Proclaiming the blood for eternity

Of His blood I do not plead

Boldness and confidence is what I read

Proclamation of that great name

The powerful blood I will PROCLAIM!!!!

A SPIRITUAL MAN

A spiritual man upright and true
Integrity and love thru and thru
Spiritual pride is not his lot
The grace of God he has sought

A spiritual man quite contagious
Against him the enemy rages
Victories are known through the land
In the power of God he must stand

A spiritual man faithful and true
With him no days are blue
A priest and king he shall be
When Jesus comes for you and me.

A GODLY WIFE

Virtuous and compassionate full of love

She is God's gift sent from above

To this woman I shall impart

Wisdom and knowledge to fill her heart

The fear of the Lord makes her just

In her, her husband does trust

To this woman I shall say

Receive my anointing this very day

I shall guide you through your life

Receive my anointing dear Godly wife

Integrity and honor are yours to stay

You shall be blessed day by day.

A GODLY HUSBAND

Prophet, Priest and a King

The Word of God he does bring

Protects and serves from a pure heart

Being a provider is but a start

He is the image and glory of the Lord

Fearlessly wielding the two edged sword

A strong, bold and powerful life

He'll gladly lay it down for his wife

Love and compassion from whom does flow

To him his wife will gladly go

A strong bridge over the pressures of life

He'll be blessed with a godly wife.

EPILOGUE

THIS BOOK IS ABOUT HEARING GOD IN A POETIC SENSE. God speaks in a variety of ways and poetry is one of them. I pray you have been as blessed by these poems as I have.

BIO

William carries the anointing of a prophet and psalmist. He is also a Bible teacher, author and international speaker. He operates in all of the Spiritual gifts. He uses the gifts as the Holy Spirit wills. One of William's great desires is to lead others to Christ and to follow Holy Spirit wherever He leads.

www.ingramcontent.com/pod-product-compliance
Lightning Source LLC
Chambersburg PA
CBHW042336150426
43195CB00001B/10